Old Orleans

MEMORIES OF A CAPE COD TOWN

Old Orleans

MEMORIES OF A CAPE COD TOWN

MARY E. McDERMOTT

Sea Crow Press
amplifying voices

Sea Crow Press

Trade Paperback ISBN: 987-1-7358140-5-6

Ebook ISBN: 978-1-7358140-6-3

Cover Design by PopKitty Design

Interior Formatting by Mary Petiet

Photographs From the Author's Collection

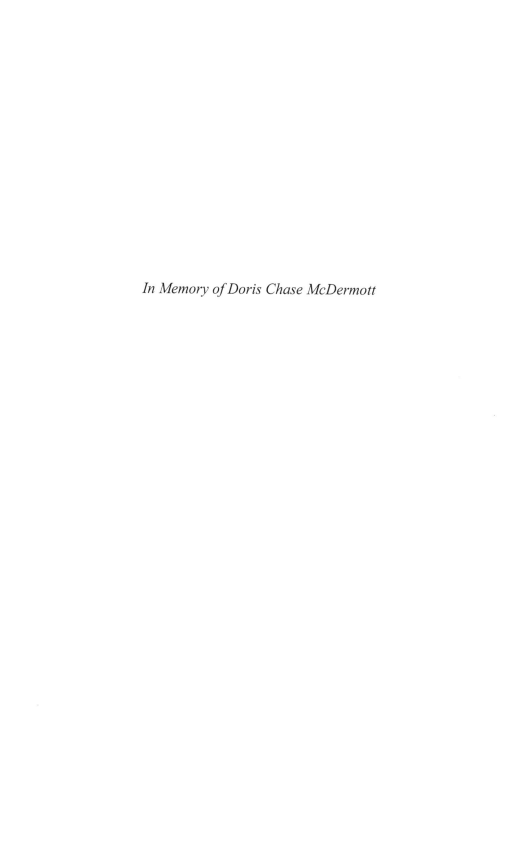

In Memory of Doris Chase McDermott

CONTENTS

INTRODUCTION

TRAVEL BACK IN TIME TO OLD ORLEANS

Having had the tremendous good fortune to be born in Orleans, and the additional good fortune to have a mother who was also born here and could tell me wonderful stories of her childhood and youth, I wanted to preserve some of those stories and share them. Very few people remain who would remember the things my mother told me about.

I also wanted to honor my aunt Alice Freeman, who played a significant role in my upbringing, and to share my own memories of the Orleans that used to be.

This collection includes two pieces of short fiction which are loosely based on stories I heard from my mother.

1

WHAT MY MOTHER KNEW

My mother, Doris Chase (later McDermott) entered the world on a Monday morning in 1912, "just in time to do the wash," as her mother said. Doris was the first baby to appear in the East Orleans neighborhood for many years, and the neighbors asked the family to hang a white sheet out the window when she was born. "I surrendered as soon as I arrived," she quipped.

Doris Chase McDermott with her sister Alice.

After Doris's birth, her mother was ill for some time, so Alice, the oldest girl in the family, was the child's main caregiver. Unable to pronounce the name "Alice," little Doris called her "Ass." This appellation caused great embarrassment when the toddler fell asleep at a movie and woke from a nightmare screaming, "Ass! Ass!"

Although childhood pictures of Doris show a pretty brunette with a sweet expression, there was definitely a less-sweet side to her personality. Her older brother had a friend, Charlie Young, who would come over to play; on the way, he would stop at a small store and buy some penny candy for Doris. On occasion, she would pout, "I don't like that kind!" and Charlie would walk back to the store and exchange it for the type she preferred. When both were senior citizens, Charlie would say, "Your mother was a brat!"

Bathing beauties. The author's mother, Doris Chase McDermott, is in front.

Her older brother, Earle, apparently shared that opinion. One day when she was pestering him, he gave her a spoon and told her to dig to China. Eventually, he said, she would see a coolie's hat going around. She dug all day but was disappointed to find herself no closer to the Orient.

The family occupied various rentals in town, notably a large house on what is now the Village Green. Doris liked the location because it was exciting to see the many fender-benders that resulted from cars speeding down the hill (there was no traffic light at the intersection in those days). She and her friend Mary Penniman (later McPhee) enjoyed rolling their hoops around Academy Place, shouting "Erdi-Erdi!" in imitation of the sound of an auto horn. She also liked to ride her bike around the same area but had to get up early to do so—otherwise, her younger brother, Wilbur, would push her off it and claim the two-wheeler for himself.

The author's mother, Doris Chase McDermott, with her bicycle.

There was a big cherry tree in the front yard. Mary delighted in climbing it until Doris's mother called, "Mary Penniman, you get down from there before you break your neck!" Doris wisely stayed on the ground.

Mr. and Mrs. Geers lived on the other side of Academy Place, in the house that most recently was the Academy Ocean Grill. They had gas pumps, and Mrs. Geers was the attendant. She kept her change in a "farmer's purse" which fit into a pocket sewed to the inside of her skirt.

Mr. Geers wore a cowboy hat and, fittingly, had a herd of cows which he pastured on the land where Friends' Marketplace is now located. Every day, Doris would see him driving the cows to and from the pasture.

A little girl named Beulah who lived on Tonset Road was given to running away, simply out of curiosity to see the world. Doris would see little Beulah toddling up Academy Place and would intercept her and walk her home. Neither of them dreamed that someday their daughters would be schoolmates.

One day, Doris and a friend both got babysitting jobs on the same afternoon. They pushed the baby carriages up Tonset Road and decided it would be fun to put the hoods down and run as fast as they could. Naturally, the babies set up a howl. Mr. Henry Colwell was sitting on his porch swing and asked what was wrong. Assuming innocent faces, the girls assured him that they had no idea. Having raised children himself, Mr. Colwell was undoubtedly on to their game; he invited them to sit on the swing with the babies. The gentle rocking motion calmed them right down, and their unsuspecting mothers were never the wiser.

Orleans had its share of entertainments. There was the movie theater (silent at first), a roller rink, and a bowling alley. Each summer, the Chautauqua would come to town and present educational shows about different cultures. There was always a parade on the first day, and one year, Doris and Mary were chosen to march in the parade as clowns. This was a big event for the little girls.

Halloween was always observed, and one October, the family had a big pumpkin on the doorstep. They were sitting in the dark that Halloween night, probably because they had nothing to give trick-or-treaters, when they saw a local boy come skulking up to the step. He was ready to grab the pumpkin when their mother intoned in her ghostliest voice, "Leave it alone! Leave it alone!" The would-be thief took off like a shot!

For some reason, the night before the Fourth of July was a traditional time for adult men to play pranks. One Fourth, Doris awoke to find a sign advertising T. A. Smith's market outside her bedroom window!

She enjoyed seeing the summer people arrive; many families would come by train and spend the entire season, while the father came on the weekends. One visitor she always looked for was Professor Watts from New Hampshire, who had a cottage on Town Cove. She recalled seeing him walking uptown, always wearing neatly pressed chinos with a light blue shirt and shoes that squeaked. Many years later, when I had a summer job at Snow Library, I met the professor, who was still wearing a blue shirt and chinos—and his shoes still squeaked!

As the youngest girl, Doris was assigned the chores that her older sisters disdained: pumping water, emptying the chamber pots, and filling the kerosene lamps and trimming the wicks. One winter evening when she was about 8, she went into the pump room to get water when the connecting door to the shed opened and a white face peeked out. Terrified, she ran back into the house. "There's a ghost out there!" she told her sister Nellie. At age 15, Nellie didn't believe in ghosts; "I'll get the water," she said scornfully. Seconds later she was back, gasping, "There *is* a ghost out there!"

The only law enforcement officer was a sheriff who lived up the hill. He was called, but took his time in arriving. He finally got there, brandishing a shotgun, saying, "Where is he? Where is he?" By then, the apparition was long gone, but in the morning, the family observed strange tracks—not human—in the snow. Perhaps someone wearing false feet had been playing a prank; they never learned the identity of their ghostly visitor.

Doris's father served in the Coast Guard for many years at several stations, mainly in Orleans and Eastham. Sometimes she would have the opportunity to spend the night at the Orleans station.

She loved falling asleep to the sound of the waves and awakening to the smell of bacon frying for breakfast.

When the schooner Montclair was wrecked off Orleans with a cargo of laths, Doris and her brother Wilbur were on the scene. It was a bitterly cold day in the winter of 1927, and she put her hands in his pockets to keep them warm. She vividly remembered seeing a man in the water waving an arm and calling for help, then sinking out of sight.

Doris Chase McDermott with her brother Wilbur.

It's hard to realize that things we take for granted today, such as cars and planes, were rarities in those days. Doris vividly recalled her first sight of an airplane. She was walking across an open field where Cooke's restaurant is now when she heard an engine and looked up to see a small plane overhead. In a panic, she threw herself to the ground and waited to be attacked! The impression must have lasted; all her life, she refused to fly. Asked if she would ever like to go to Europe, she said, "Yes, if there were a bridge and I could take a bus!"

There were no streetlights in town until Mrs. Anna Rogers Coffin and her friends organized the Hen Hawk Society to raise money for the installation of gas lights. The Chase siblings used to watch eagerly each evening for the arrival of Joshua Northup, whom they called "Leerie the Lamplighter" after the character in Robert Louis Stevenson's poem. Mr. Northup would unfold his ladder, climb up, and light the gas lamp in front of the house.

Orleans had no snowplows then, and the road crews had to shovel the streets by hand. Central heating was still uncommon, and the Chase family used to bank the house with seaweed in the winter as a form of exterior insulation. At bedtime, the children would warm themselves by the stove, then dash upstairs and jump into bed in their unheated bedrooms.

Doris and Nellie shared a bedroom, and one winter, they also shared scarlet fever. The house had quarantine signs posted on the doors, and their library books had to be burned to avoid spreading the disease. Nellie was the sicker of the two. Dr. Lodge from Brewster attended the girls, and he knew the crisis for Nellie would come around midnight on a certain night. He promised to be there and started out to drive, but a snowstorm was raging and his car got stuck at the Orleans line. The doctor got out and walked the rest of the way. (As Doris often remarked, "Nowadays they won't even make a house call on a sunny day!") Nellie survived, although her hair fell out. It grew back in due time. Doris was left with a cough that kept both girls awake for many nights and made Nellie want to strangle her. She was finally prescribed a lozenge that numbed her throat and got rid of the cough.

All 12 grades of the Orleans school were located in the same building, on the site where the former American Legion Hall now stands. Doris enjoyed the slide on the playground, but her mother forbade her to use it while wearing her good school clothes. She had to walk home after school, change into her sateen bloomers, then walk back to the school to use the slide. As she recalled, there was time for only one or two slides before she was due at home for supper.

School lunches were cooked by Mr. Hopkins in the basement cafeteria; Doris always looked forward to his Irish stew—although she did not look forward to rats running across her feet as she descended the stairs!

The faculty were an interesting group. The principal, Herbert "Pop" Stewart, liked to poke his head into a classroom while the teacher's back was turned and make funny faces. When the students burst into laughter, the teacher always took it personally and refused to believe Mr. Stewart would do such a silly thing. Miss Snow, the home economics teacher, used to emphasize the importance of practice by saying, "Do it again and again!" When Doris got the thread tangled up in the sewing machine, she was terrified of what Miss Snow would say, but an older girl helped her untangle the mess before it was discovered. Some teachers were quirky, like Miss Arnaud, who would send Doris to her house to feed her cats, and others were downright frightening, like Mr. Buck, who didn't mind throwing his cane at a disobedient pupil.

She had ambitions to become a nurse, but that goal was not to be achieved. At age 14, she was trying to button her shoes in preparation for school when a button flew off and she collapsed in tears. Sensing that something more than frustration about a button was behind the outburst, her mother took her to a doctor, who said, "Don't send that girl to school any more." Many years later, I asked if something at school had been bothering her, but she did not remember.

Diagonally across the street from the Chase home was a hill upon which sat the Eagle Wing Hotel. There were two stone pillars flanking a flight of steps which ascended from the street to the hotel. En route to the movies as teenagers, Doris and her brother Wilbur used to hide behind the pillars and sneak a smoke.

Getting her driver's license was a major milestone for Doris. An older friend taught her to drive; she practiced three-point turns on Route 28 in the area known as "the plains," near where the Orleans watershed is today. She got a little Ford with a rumble seat and enjoyed taking her mother for rides. On one occasion, they invited her mother's cousin Minnie along. "Aunt Minnie" was a lady of ample proportions and got stuck in the rumble seat! It took the combined efforts of Doris and her mother to free Minnie.

The author's mother, Doris Chase McDermott.

Doris came into her own when she went to work for the telephone company, as her three older sisters had also at various times. (Alice made it her career.) She loved being in the middle of whatever excitement was going on in town. The operators not only connected calls: they accepted payments for phone bills; tested the fire whistle daily; and blew the whistle and called all the firefighters in the event of a fire. On one occasion, she saved the life of an elderly woman. Upon answering the signal, she heard only a moan on the other end of the line. She located a doctor and dispatched him to the woman's home. He found her bleeding profusely after

accidentally cutting herself while chopping vegetables. She
survived, and Doris was written up in the Central Cape Press newspaper for saving the woman's life.

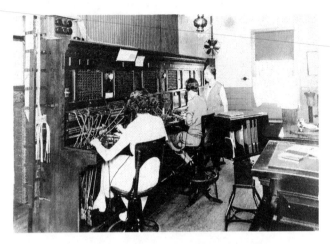

The Orleans Telephone Office.

The telephone office originally operated on a "drop" system;
each number was assigned to a metal drop, and when a call was
placed from that number, the drop fell down. When the operator
answered, she pushed the drop back into place with a wooden
implement. Eventually, the operation was changed to a light system,
with a number's light coming on when that person wished to make a
call.

Doris and her co-worker Hilda Young were to ride to Chatham
with the district supervisor, "Miss K," to be trained on the new
system. The night before the scheduled training session, a "cutover
party" was held at the Southward Inn, and liquid refreshment
abounded. Doris and Hilda were horrified to see Miss K sitting on
the stairs holding her head after one too many toasts.

The next day, the trio set out for Chatham in the supervisor's
car. When the rear door was opened, a gust of wind caught it and
"sprung" it so it wouldn't stay closed. On the way to Chatham,

Hilda held on to the door and Doris held on to Hilda. On the way back, they reversed positions.

Once they arrived in Chatham, Miss K decamped to the lounge to nurse her hangover, leaving the two operators to learn as best they could by observation. Somehow they managed, and they were grateful to get back to Orleans unscathed.

One year, the telephone company had a float in the Fourth of July parade. Doris was seated at a table with a mock switchboard, and lineman Kimball Coombs was standing by a telephone pole. No one had noticed that the chair in which Doris sat was on casters, and when the truck began to move, she nearly slid right off the back. She sat with her legs wrapped around the table leg for the entire parade!

Social life in those days centered around dances, movies, and the soda shop. "Going steady" was not as common then; people would attend dances in groups. Doris and her sisters would hire a taxi to take them to a dance, and their mother would go along. Doris didn't know whether to be amused or incensed when a young man asked her mother to dance (she declined) but did not ask Doris! She enjoyed dancing, particularly doing a fast foxtrot. Some young men were excellent dancers, while others were like the fellow who pumped her arm so constantly that she half expected to see water gushing.

Parents seem to have been stricter in those days. Doris recalled sitting on the porch, talking to a boy, when his irate mother came storming up the street, grabbed him by the ear, and marched him home to do his chores.

Playing pinball was a popular pastime, and Doris proved to be a "natural" at it. She and Dr. Henry A White, who called her "Minnie Mouse," met regularly for pinball competitions at a local store after his office hours.

Doris had her share of dates but did not become serious about anyone until she met Eddie McDermott, who had come from Boston to work at a local supermarket. He was a sharp dresser with an easy charm, and she was smitten. He already had a fiancée in Boston, hand-picked by his older sister, but he apparently relished the opportunity to make his own choice. He and Doris became engaged, but every time he went home, he was racked with indecision. She finally delivered an ultimatum: marry or break up. They were married on June 10, 1934. Their honeymoon consisted of one night at a Hyannis hotel; both had to work the next day, he in Boston.

The author's parents as a young married couple.

One of the first meals Doris cooked for her new husband featured asparagus. After eating the stalks, he said, "That's good. I'll have some more," to which she replied that there was no more. "What about the tips?" he asked. "Oh," she said, "I didn't think those were any good, so I threw them away." She learned, however, and became a good cook who made hearty, comforting dishes.

The couple lived in apartments for a few years while saving up to buy a house. They eventually purchased a lot on South Orleans Road and built a one-and-a-half-story Cape with a detached garage. The original plans included dormers and a breezeway, but when she wondered why neither materialized, the builders told her, "Oh, your husband said not to do those." An elderly retired mason lived up the street, and every day he would walk down to watch the builders work. His persistent presence began to drive them crazy, so they agreed to let him build the fireplace and chimney. To Doris's horror, much of the brickwork reflected his unsteadiness, and she insisted that the part of the chimney which was visible in the living room be enclosed in pine above the mantel.

The night the Hurricane of 1944 was forecast to hit, Doris had just finished her shift at the telephone office. When her replacement came on duty, she offered to stay with him, but he said, "No, no, go home. We're not going to get anything." As soon as she walked into the house, he called and implored, "Come back! The board is lit up like a Christmas tree!" Eddie had garaged the car and refused to take it out again, so she called the local Civil Defense office for a ride. The board was indeed lit up; she tried to answer a call and got an electric shock. The two operators had no way of knowing which lights signified calls and which were simply the result of the storm. They called their local technician, Cecil Mayo, and he set off on foot from his home on Tonset Road. It was dawn when he finally arrived after a night of walking through back yards and dodging trees and downed wires. The wind had been so strong that a large tree just outside the telephone office had blown down and neither operator had heard it.

Doris had a lot of wisdom and was very perceptive about people. She became close to a younger colleague at the telephone office who was dating an older man she expected to marry. When his engagement to someone else was suddenly announced, she arrived at Doris's home in tears. Doris counseled her, "If he's not a truthful man, he's not a man you could be happy with." The disappointed young woman later met a man with whom she had a long and happy marriage.

Doris looked forward to becoming a mother but was unable to get pregnant until 1945. Eddie was working in Provincetown and liked to go out for a few drinks at the Flagship or the Lobster Pot after work. Doris would take the bus down to Provincetown after finishing her shift at the telephone office and would join him, keeping her alcohol intake minimal in order to drive home. She encountered several notable visitors at the popular night spots: she saw Anaïs Nin, met Helena Rubinstein, and danced with Dr. Scholl. She said he was so short, she could have eaten off his head.

One early morning, she was driving home while Eddie slept; in Eastham, the car was enveloped in a thick fog. As the fog lifted, she saw a line of bicyclists, swerved to avoid them, and hit a telephone pole. Her face struck the wooden steering wheel, breaking both the wheel and her jaw, as well as knocking out her front teeth. Within a couple of months, she was pregnant. "Had I known that was the answer," she said, "I would have hit a pole a long time ago."

Although Doris had loved her job, she gave it up to become a full-time mother. Her doctor predicted twins, and she happily bought two sets of baby clothes, one in pink and one in blue, hoping for a girl and a boy. On the Fourth of July, 1946, she began having pains. Eddie found her doctor at the baseball game; the doctor later jokingly complained about having been taken away from the best ball game of the season. He said, "Get going to the hospital and don't stop to pick any daisies on the way!"

Once at the hospital, Doris found herself on a cot in the corridor, waiting . . . and waiting. They had picked up Alice on the way; the nervous father-to-be kept saying, "Let's go get a cup of coffee," and Alice later said she had never drunk so much coffee in her life!

At 1:30 AM on July 5, I made my appearance as a solo act. When my mother regained consciousness, she looked at me through an anesthetic fog and lamented, "Oh no, I had a fish!" When clarity returned, she asked about the other twin and was told she had given birth to only one child. For many years afterward, she wondered if the second twin had been given to someone else! She wrapped up the blue items and mailed them to her sister Nellie, who was pregnant, with a note saying, "Have a baby shower all by yourself!" Nellie gave birth to a son!

The doctor advised Doris not to have another child for at least two years; in 1950, she had to have a complete hysterectomy, which ended any chance of further pregnancies. She was horrified that her husband asked the parish priest if it was all right for her to have the surgery! In those days, a hysterectomy was a far more invasive procedure than it is today, and she had a long convalescence.

From this point on in my narrative, I shall refer to Doris as Mother, because that was a role she relished and at which she excelled. I was (and still am) extremely stubborn, so she had her work cut out for her. Sometimes she had to resort to desperate measures. When I resisted taking a bath, she scared me into cleanliness by saying that if my feet got too dirty, they would fall off. My recalcitrance about eating vegetables was met with the dire prediction that my bones would turn to jelly and my blood to water. Veggies suddenly became very appealing! On one occasion, she resorted to the threat of reform school; whatever I had been doing, I stopped doing in a hurry!

Mother also had a keen understanding of child psychology. Once I declared that I was going to go out and eat worms. She calmly replied, "All right, go out and find a worm and take a good look at it and think about whether you want to eat it." I immediately rescinded my decision.

When I packed a few items in a bandana and announced my intention of running away, she said, "If that's what you really want to do, I won't try to stop you. Just remember that if you're out in the woods, there won't be anything to eat, and there will be wild animals out there." I decided to give her one more chance!

Mother was a natural with animals of any species; she could get catbirds to eat raisins from her hand, and she taught me to do it also. The secret was to be quiet and patient.

I loved to hear Mother sing funny songs like "Pistol-Packin' Mama," "Barney Google," and "Cement Mixer." She was patience itself with my requests for repeated playing of records such as "McNamara's Band" and "Who Threw the Overalls in Mrs. Murphy's Chowder?"

At the time Mother worked for the telephone company, her male co-worker was engaged to the woman whom he later married. He sometimes received packages of divinity fudge which Mother assumed had been made by his fiancée, and he always shared it. When I started first grade, my teacher turned out to be his wife, and Mother complimented her on the candy. She replied frostily, "I have never made divinity fudge in my life!" I'll bet she found out who did, though!

Mother was my anchor through bullying, anorexia, teen angst, and so much more. She welcomed my friends into our home; there was always room for one more at the table. Her sense of humor won many hearts. My best high school friend, Dennis Marsh, said she reminded him of the British comic actress Hermione Gingold. One evening, she walked into the living room wearing a wig in Hermione's signature red color, holding a cigar like the actress smoked, and murmured, "Hello, dahling," in a throaty British accent. It was the only time I ever saw Dennis at a loss for words!

My parents separated in 1959 but remained friends for life. Mother summoned her reserves of strength and courage to survive some difficult times. It was not always easy to make ends meet, so Mother took in ironing. Her work was impeccable, and one customer said it rivaled that of the luxury laundries in New York.

One summer, a man who was working at the A&P rented a room down the street from us, and he needed some clothes ironed. Our next-door neighbor at that time had a lively sense of curiosity. She saw the man arrive at the back door with an overnight bag, which held his ironing, but did not see him leave through the front door and walk to work. Sure he had spent the night, she arose early the next morning, placed her lawn chair in the backyard, and watched our back door for hours!

Mother also got a pamphlet on making candles with paraffin and created many unusual and lovely candles. She sold some through Ellis' Market (the kindly owner, Lloyd Ellis, would not take a commission) and some privately to friends. Others, she gave as gifts.

Whenever someone had a birthday or other occasion for celebration, Mother could be counted on to bake and decorate a cake. I remember as a child hearing her say she was going to bake a cake for George Washington's birthday. Unsure who he was, I asked hesitantly if we were going to eat it. She responded merrily, "Sure! You didn't think I was going to give it to George Washington, did you?" The cake appeared every February thereafter: fudge cake with fudge frosting and maraschino cherries on top. I still salivate at the memory!

In my senior year of college, my dorm had a Christmas party and the residents contributed various snacks. Mother sent me back from Thanksgiving vacation with 54 bite-size fruit cakes, one for each person in the dorm. They won rave reviews, but I foolishly didn't attend the party because I was brooding over whether my boyfriend loved me (he didn't). I still regret missing the fun.

Mother was wonderful at dealing with death, always able to put her own grief on the back burner and do what had to be done, while others around her were falling apart. She never forced me to go to a visitation or a funeral. I was very fond of her mother, who died when I was 15. Given the choice to attend the service or not, I chose not to. After the funeral, Mother came home and told me about the service, describing the flowers and naming the people who were there. That was a very comforting conversation. The family was gathering at my Aunt Alice's house for lunch, so I went there with her and felt better being around my cousins and hearing everyone talk normally. (I hadn't been sure how one conversed under the circumstances.) I ate with my older cousin Sonny, who talked about the importance of education and his regret at not having finished school. That conversation had a big impact on my thinking. After lunch, Mother took me to the cemetery to see the flowers, and that too was a comforting experience.

The first time Mother took me to a visitation, it was for a friend of hers whom I had not known, so there was no grief on my part. It was an excellent introduction to the funeral experience. Years later, I found that I had been blessed with Mother's ability to remain calm under such circumstances, and that I was able to speak at funeral services.

Mother's method of grieving, I learned upon the deaths of Aunt Alice and Uncle Wilbur, was to get up in the middle of the night, drink coffee, and smoke cigarettes with the radio on very low. She would do this for several nights while she worked through her feelings.

Always supportive, Mother guided but didn't push. Unlike many of my classmates, I was not pressured to go to college; the decision was mine. When I decided to go, I had her full support. She encouraged me in my studies, sent weekly letters full of local newspaper clippings, and welcomed my college friends for visits. Once when a few of my classmates and I were fooling around with a Ouija board, I asked it the name of the first boy I would date in college. Someone was obviously pushing the planchette, for the answer came up as "Clem Walnut"! Laughing, I wrote about it to Mother; in her next letter, she enclosed a few dollars and said, "If you see Clem Walnut, buy him a soda."

Many of the expressions Mother used are rarely heard today, but they were too colorful to be forgotten. Surprise would be conveyed by, "heavens to Betsy and eight hands around!" or disgust by "ye gods and little fishhooks!" Something insignificant "didn't amount to Hannah Cook," and a minor inconvenience that did no harm was "no kill-cat." A chewy piece of meat was "tougher than white oak."

A person who might today be described as a few sandwiches short of a picnic was "only six ounces to the pound," while someone who appeared thin and pale looked "like a picked gull" or "like he'd been dragged through a knothole."

If Mother herself wasn't feeling up to par, she felt "all mops and brooms" or "mopsy-broomsy" and "didn't care whether school kept or not." If she were confused, she didn't know whether she "was foot or horseback." A glance in the mirror on a bad day evoked the dismayed exclamation, "I look like I'd been sent for and was just comin'!" A messy room looked "like it was goin' for a ride."

Longtime acquaintances were people she had known "since Hector was a pup." An inquiry into a third party's mental state or behavior might be, "how's he carryin' sail?", especially if said person was known for being "three sheets to the wind" or "over the bay" (drunk). If someone had a particularly ruddy countenance, his face was "like the rising sun." (This blush was usually the result of being "three sheets to the wind.") A person she considered spineless was "just like a jellyfish." Her version of "consider the source" was "what can you expect from a pig but a grunt?" Her variation on "insult added to injury" was "worse and more *of* it!"

With her generous nature, she sometimes "cooked enough for a fish crew" and might "cut cross-lots" on her way to share some of the bounty with a neighbor.

Mother had an excellent rapport with children; when she was recovering from rheumatoid arthritis, several neighborhood boys would stop by to bring in her newspaper and chat. She was a good listener, and they appreciated an attentive ear. One boy enjoyed fishing, and Mother mentioned that she preferred fish to steak. A few days later, he appeared at the door with some fish he had caught and which his father had filleted. He always remembered their friendship; when she passed away at the age of 91, he and his mother came to the visitation at the funeral home. By that time, he was a grown man, and it was with tremendous sorrow that I paid a condolence call on his mother after his own death just a few years later.

Mother had become a nervous driver by the time I was born; the Eastham accident had been her second, following too closely after a collision in Sandwich. The other party was at fault in the Sandwich mishap, but he blamed Mother and they ended up in court. After his attorney shook his finger at her while asking a question, she told the judge she would answer when the lawyer got out of her face. The judge ordered the attorney to step back, the other party admitted under cross-examination to having been in a rush at the time of the accident, and the case was dismissed.

From the time of the Eastham crash, Mother would drive no farther than Brewster on one side and Eastham on the other, and those only when absolutely necessary. I had a hard time learning to drive, perhaps having absorbed some of her fear. When I finally got my license at age 38, she swore she would never ride with me, but one evening she had no choice. She was going to a Grange meeting and no one else was available to take her, so she reluctantly agreed to ride with me. She had to take a bunch of flowers for her part in the meeting, so as she got seated in the car, she joked, "Well, if anything happens, I've got my flowers!" It wasn't long before she was a regular passenger with me, to our mutual delight. Once when I was going somewhere with friends, she remarked, "I hope you're doing the driving"; that was a high compliment indeed!

Mother was a strong and patient woman who had the wisdom to respond to difficult circumstances with reason instead of anger, and a positive attitude that helped her to find the bright side of a dark situation. Even in her last years, after the loss of her central vision, when she was living in a nursing home, she was gracious to everyone. She always thanked the nurses and aides for anything they did for her. As her friend Mary Jane Gibson commented, "She had elegant manners."

It would take volumes to detail what my mother knew, but the most important things were kindness, generosity, and love.

2

AUNT ALICE

*W*e've all heard of the woman who could bring home the bacon and fry it up in the pan. Well, my aunt Alice could dig the clams, shuck 'em right there on the flats, bring 'em home, and make chowder. There wasn't much she couldn't do.

The author's aunt, Alice Myrtle Chase.

Alice Myrtle Chase was born in East-ham, Massachusetts, on October 20, 1897, the first child of my grandfather Wilbur Curtis Chase and grandmother Nellie Baker Ramsey, who had been married the previous December. Five younger siblings followed over the next 18 years; as the family grew, the Chases moved to larger rentals, most of them in Orleans.

Grandpa served in the US Life Saving Service, later part of the Coast Guard, so he was usually at home only one day per week. The work was dangerous and the pay meager.

Occasionally, the government would send surplus food to the Coast Guardsmen; Aunt Alice recalled that Grandpa once brought home some cheese, which he intended to share with his mother. Grandma felt that he was putting his mother (who disliked her) before his children. "It turned her head," Alice said, "and she ran off into the swamp."

Grandma made all the children's clothes except shoes; the latter required a train trip to the shoe store in Harwich. Alice had to leave school and work to bring in some additional income; she worked at a bakery in East Orleans until she was needed at home to care for her youngest siblings when their mother was ill. She became a second mother to Doris and Wilbur Jr, who were 15 and 18 years younger, respectively.

Alice seemed to have a natural immunity to childhood diseases; she nursed her siblings through measles, mumps, and even scarlet fever without contracting any of the ailments.

She worked as a telephone operator in Orleans, excelled at the work, and enjoyed it. Once, when she had some time off, she went to Boston and stayed at the Statler Hotel. On the weekend, Doris took the train up to join her. Doris had fallen on the back doorstep and badly scraped her knee; she always remembered sitting in the hotel bathroom while Alice bandaged her knee!

Alice was an active Grange member, attending meetings in various Cape towns. At a meeting of the Brewster Grange, she met

John Freeman, a cranberry grower and retired mining engineer who had worked in California, South Africa, and Siberia, where he barely escaped with his life during the Bolshevik Revolution. She and John began dating, much to Grandma's consternation: John was 30 years older than Alice and had been divorced.

John and Alice became engaged despite Grandma's fears that Alice would become "a bird in a gilded cage," in the words of a popular song of the era. One day, Alice asked Grandma and my mother, Doris, to accompany her to Hyannis to buy a dress for that night's Grange supper and installation ceremony. On the way home, she announced, "Well, I might as well tell you: John and I are getting married tonight."

Alice's fellow Granger and close friend Addie Hassard lived next door to the Brewster Town Hall, where the activities were to take place. During the intermission between the supper and the installation, Alice went over to Addie's house to "freshen up." John Freeman left the hall quietly and met them. By prearrangement, the minister arrived and they exchanged vows, then returned to the Grange as husband and wife.

The Freemans were married for seven years, during which time John became ill and Alice assumed management of his cranberry bogs and blueberry bushes. When a frost was forecast, she had to call the hired man in Harwich to come and flood the bogs to protect them. Alice proved to be a highly capable manager as well as an excellent cook. During his travels, John had acquired a taste for highly spiced food, and their table sported a lazy susan filled with bottles of various hot sauces and spices.

According to my mother, John was a rather controlling husband; if Alice wanted to drive to New Bedford for a shopping trip, she had to wait until John had heard EB Rideout's weather forecast on the radio and decided if it was safe for her to go or not.

After John's death, Alice sold the agricultural properties and accepted a position as chief operator of the Brewster telephone office. She came to know a lot about Brewster families, both year-round and seasonal residents. She told of one family who summered in Brewster and had a son who did not want to return to college. His parents insisted that he do so, and one evening Alice heard him running down Main Street and screaming. Unfortunately, she never heard what ultimately happened to the young man.

In those days, the high school senior classes were small enough to be rewarded with a trip to Washington, DC. Alice was asked to act as chaperone for the Brewster seniors at least once, and also accompanied the Orleans graduating class in the same capacity when she lived in Orleans. She recalled walking down the hotel corridor and spotting an Orleans boy—later a well-known local businessman—without a stitch on, desperately pounding on the door of his room. While he had been in the shower, his roommates had taken his clothes and towel, then pushed him out into the hall when he emerged.

When the chief operator position opened up in the Orleans office, Alice took it and moved back home to help her mother and her brother Wilbur, who lived in the same house. The telephone office was ideally located just a short distance away, so if she were working a split shift, she could go home for lunch and also cook dinner.

Having no children of her own, Alice delighted in spoiling her many nieces and nephews. When I was very young, I expressed a desire for "an angel girl" to go on the top of the Christmas tree. Alice bought me a beautiful paper angel with a halo of spun glass, which graced the tree for many years to come. She would often stop by at the holidays with some treat such as a gingerbread man or a kit for making styrofoam ornaments.

Aunt Alice's bedroom was a treasure trove of fascinating items, and I always loved being invited to explore it with her. Usually, she would give me some trinket that I would treasure for years: a pair of Scottie dog pins engraved, "souvenir of Washington, DC"; a filigree heart pendant with blue stones; a piggy-bank charm with a penny embedded in its back. I can still smell the subtle fragrance of perfume and powder that always pervaded her room.

The author as a toddler with her Aunt Alice.

Aunt Alice was my role model when I was a child. I saw her as the perfect example of an independent woman; she had a job, drove a car, dug clams, and was the only person in the family who could set a mousetrap without catching her finger! As an adult, I see that she was not as independent as I had thought; she was bound by her sense of obligation to both her mother and her brother.

After her mother's death, she continued to feel responsible for her brother's well-being and made a home for him until her own death. Her life was one of service to her family and friends, and I try to emulate her kindness as best I can.

3

GROWING UP AS A BABY BOOMER
IN ORLEANS

*O*ne of my first memories is of going to the Fourth of July parade, which always wound up at Eldredge Park, just down the street from our house. I loved the music, the marching units, and the elaborate floats. One year, the overhead sign with the name of the park had to be taken down so a tall float could fit under it. After the parade, there would be games and races for the kids, a practice which has now been discontinued, probably for liability reasons. They had the three-legged race, the Dizzy Izzy race, and several others.

The author behind her grandmother's house. The bog in the background is now a Stop & Shop.

Baseball games at the park were as popular then as now, although they were always held in daylight because the field had no lights at that time. I went to one game with my father when I was about four or five. The field had bleachers then, and we sat on the top one; there was a backrest, but I was too short for my head to reach it. My father sat on one side of me, and a family friend, Henry Hurley, came and sat on the other. Not too far into the game, I slipped right under the backrest and fell; I remember seeing both men turn around and grab for me, but they were too late. Down I went, just missing the water faucet behind the bleachers. My father carried me home, bleeding and crying, and my mother vowed, "She's never going anywhere with you again!"

I was born at 1:30 AM on July fifth, but we used to celebrate my birthday on the fourth. Mother would borrow our neighbor Estelle Thompson's dining room chairs; the two ladies would go back and forth across the street carrying chairs. (There was less traffic on Route 28 in those days!) My godmother, Bea Linnell, would come to help with the party preparations; her husband would drop her off and would go to the annual horse show at Mayo's Field. When he picked her up, we would all have supper together.

My father used to keep a big box of potato chips next to his chair for munching while he watched television. One party guest, whose parents must not have allowed such snacks, discovered the box and carried it around with her all afternoon, crunching happily. My mother warned her mother to be alert for signs of an upset stomach!

I loved dolls, and Uncle Wilbur built me a doll bed whose foundation was made of rope my Grandpa Chase had braided when he was in the Coast Guard. Grandma Chase made the mattress, pillow, and a patchwork quilt for it. I still have the doll bed; the braided rope is a treasure because it was worked by the grandfather I never knew.

Uncle Wilbur also built me a desk with storage space and a lid that opened. He could make or repair just about anything. He was a gifted storyteller, and he enjoyed taking pictures. Had circumstances been different, I think he could have made a fine writer or photojournalist, or a finish carpenter.

My parents enjoyed listening to records. Some of the songs they played are never heard now: "When You and I Were Young, Maggie"; "When You Wore a Tulip (and I Wore a Red, Red Rose)"; and a song that, for some reason, I hate: "Cruising Down the River." But I still love Glenn Miller, especially "In the Mood," and John Philip Sousa.

Orleans was not the bustling town then that it is now, but there were some great stores that I still miss. Robinson's 5 and 10 had everything from candles to canning supplies, from dish towels to diaries. Temple's hardware store also carried a little of everything. Mr. Temple's daughter used to paint vases in colorful swirling patterns; the vases were placed on yardsticks to dry, and the customer received a free vase—and yardstick—with every purchase. In the same building with Temple's were the movie theatre and the Orleans Pharmacy.

The town's other pharmacy, Livingston's, was across the alley from the First National. Both pharmacies had soda fountains, although the one at the Orleans Pharmacy was larger and featured sandwiches and soups as well as ice cream. Those "regulars" who drank a certain number of coffees at the Orleans Pharmacy had mugs reserved for them, inscribed with their names and hung on a pegboard. I believe the first patron to achieve that honor was Alzero "Al" Brown, who was in charge of putting up the letters on the theatre marquee. On one occasion, the "P" letters were broken, so the featured film was "RETURN OF THE INK ANTHER."

Main Street boasted the Denise Ann Bake Shop, named for the owner's daughter. To walk in the door was to smell paradise. Ernie Saulnier was known for his lemon butterfly cupcakes, made of yellow cake with lemon filling on top, adorned with two delicate cake "wings" dusted with powdered sugar. Ernie made huge butter-crunch cookies with butterscotch candies and nuts; brownies; cakes; and all manner of pastry delights. My grandmother favored a lemon chiffon pie with a graham cracker crust and a decorative swirl of toasted coconut on top.

Dorrie's store was a fun place to visit, with a lunch counter, baked goods, paperback books, some groceries, etc. Mr. Dorrie was always smoking a cigar with a long ash on it; when he bent over to scoop ice cream, we all held our breath, wondering whose vanilla cone would have unexpected sprinkles! Amazingly, the ashes never fell. Mrs. Dorrie also worked there, as did Ernie Borso, a pleasant man who later managed a Western Auto store.

The post office was next to Dorrie's, in the building which now houses Vintage in Vogue. I can still smell the wonderful aroma of paper and antiquity. Sometimes there was the excitement of a pack-age, and each week there was a quirky little free newspaper called the Oracle, which was supported by advertising. (If my father got the mail, he threw the Oracle away, but my mother always kept it.) I liked the advertising with cartoons by the publisher, Ed Smith, and the paper's motto, "Never Smarter Than You Are."

Around 1958, the post office moved to Lowell Square; I think it occupied the space which now houses a yoga studio. Later still, it moved to its present location at 56 Main Street, but it has never again had that magic smell!

Going to the movies was always a treat. Florence Wilcox, the theater owner's wife, used to sit out front in the little box office and sell tickets. There were often two screenings in an evening; it was fun to sit on a bench and watch the folks leaving one or going to the other. At Christmastime, there would be a free matinee for kids, usually a Western, with free candy.

The old Snow's store was nothing like the wonderland of today, but it was uniquely delightful. I can still hear the creak of the old wooden floors. Hardware was to the right as one entered; stationery, books, and toys were to the left. Housewares were in the basement. Henry Hurley worked in hardware, and his daughter, Clarice Talkington, worked in the office. Irene DuCharme presided over the left side of the store, assisted by Wes Wilbur. Marie Tuscan managed the basement until her retirement.

The A&P, where my father worked, was at one end of Main Street, and the First National was at the other. When the A&P staff got a summer worker, usually a high school or college student, the poor kid would be told, "The guys at the First National borrowed our shelf stretcher and we need it back. Go down and ask them for it." Invariably, the obedient worker went. Also invariably, the First National guys would say, "We returned that months ago. Tell 'em to look harder." An alternative ploy was to send the victim to Snow's or Temple's for a gallon of blue and white striped paint. Again, the young man always went.

Visitors to the A&P were greeted with the heavenly aroma of fresh-roasted coffee from the grinders at the end of the cash registers. A shopper would choose either Eight O'Clock coffee in the red bag, Red Circle in the yellow, or Bokar, "vigorous and winey," in the black. The cashier would ask, "Drip or perk?", the customer would indicate the preferred grind, and the cashier would grind the beans.

Because my father worked at the A&P, my mother wasn't allowed to shop at the First National. It was an adventure to go there with Aunt Alice and see different brands. Aunt Alice used a brand of evaporated milk called Silver Cow, and I thought that was a funny name.

One of my favorite stores was the old Ellis' Market on Cove Road. We didn't often shop there, but it was always a treat when we did. I thought Ellis' was very exotic because they carried unusual items like Twinings tea and SS Pierce canned goods. I loved the creaky floors and the friendly employees. Lloyd Ellis, the owner, had taken over the store from his father-in-law, T A Smith. Lloyd was a kind man; when my mother learned to make candles, he gave her space to display them in the store and would not take a commission.

There was a comforting continuity about some things back then. We knew that every day, regardless of the weather, Harold Crowell would walk from his Pond Road home, lunch box in hand, to work at the Rich cranberry bogs off Namskaket Road; at the end of the day, he would walk back home.

The Gravems up the street had a Great Dane named Sheba. Every few days, Sheba would walk gracefully down the road to the A&P, where a butcher would give her a bone. We used to love watching her heading home with the meaty prize in her mouth.

Some neighbors rented rooms in the summer to the waitresses from Howard Johnson's. It was very comforting to lie in bed at night and hear the closing of car doors as the waitresses returned from work. This Howard Johnson's, which was seasonal, was the first franchised location outside the Quincy area and was operated by Reginald and Gladys Sprague, who were friends of Mr. Johnson. This was the place to go for an ice cream cone in then-exotic flavors like pistachio or mocha chip.

Meals in those days were simple; the evening meal was usually called supper, and the noon meal was either lunch or dinner. Mother made some excellent casseroles featuring ground beef or tuna; salmon loaf with white sauce, which I didn't like; spaghetti sauce, which I did; and on Fridays, always fried fish. Fruit salad came from a can, and Jell-O played a prominent role in both salads and desserts.

I always got my slippers at the old HK Cummings store, founded by the photographer of so many Orleans scenes. The store sold a wonderfully comfortable type of quilted slippers called "Quilt-Eez," which I believe were made in Eastham. I do not remember Mr. Cummings, but my mother recalled that if he did not have a particular item in stock, he would say, "They don't make that anymore."

Watson's was the place to go for special occasion clothes, such as an Easter hat and gloves. It was also where I got my first suede shoes, a handsome shade of brown. My mother always bought baby gifts there, usually a pair of tiny shoes with accompanying socks.

The original Snow Library was located in the center of Academy Place. My mother recalled going there as a child, when it was presided over by HK Cummings's sister Mary, whom she found intimidating. The next librarian was Ruth Barnard, who was very pleasant. I went there once, at age 5 or 6, with my Aunt Alice; I remember the amber light streaming through the windows, and I remember the book I borrowed. It was called "Jelly and George," the story of a friendship between a cat named George and a mouse who took his name from the label on a jar of jelly. I do not remember the night the library burned down, but I do remember feeling sad that the book I had enjoyed was probably reduced to ashes.

The elementary school was located where the Town Hall is now. There were two playgrounds, one for the lower three grades and one for the upper three. We had morning and afternoon recess, both of which were eagerly anticipated. It was very exciting, as a fourth-grader, to be able to use the "big kids'" playground!

Games were not my forte. To my friends' disgust, I was a total failure at skipping rope; my feet always got tangled up. I remember the nonsensical rhymes we used as we skipped: "Up and down Jamaica where the streets are made of glass/I stepped into a lady's house and there I met a lass/Her name is [insert name]/Catch her if you can/For she's in love with [insert boy's name] and he's a famous man." And this gem: "Apple on a stick/Makes me sick/Makes my stomach do two-four-six/Not because it's dirty/Not because it's clean/But because I kissed the guy/Behind the submarine."

The third-graders used to taunt the younger ones with this rhyme: "First grade babies/Second grade bums/Third grade angels/Pickin' up plums."

The first time I went on the slide, I panicked and held onto the sides. I can still see the teacher's face looking up at me as she said, "But you've got to come down, Mary Ellen."

After my first day of first grade, my mother asked eagerly, "Well, how did you like it?" To her dismay, I replied, "Not very much. I don't think I'll go again."

An early reader, I was bored with the slow progress through Dick and Jane, but reading ahead was a cardinal sin. After my mother explained the situation to my teacher, it was ascertained that I read on a seventh-grade level, and the teacher occasionally allowed me to read to the class.

Being an early reader had its disadvantages, however. My teacher assumed that I should be equally advanced in all areas and could not understand my struggles with penmanship or my total inability to make a credible paper snowflake.

We started each day with the Lord's Prayer, a Bible reading, the Pledge of Allegiance, and a patriotic song. But no one explained what we were singing about, and in first grade we didn't have songbooks until everyone could read. "America the Beautiful" was a huge mystery to me. What were "for spacious skies?" And "amber waves of grain" or "purple mountain majesties?" And what the heck was a "fruited plain?" I was similarly puzzled by the national anthem, having no idea what a "donderly light" was, much less how to see by it.

I was probably the quietest child in the class, not because I was especially virtuous but simply because I didn't want to be scolded. One month, our class had the highest attendance at PTA meetings, so we were told we would have a party. I was excited, thinking a party meant we could run around and make noise, but it just meant that we got ice cream and lollipops!

In first grade, we learned to print, using pencils. I remember being kept in at recess to practice my letters on the day the penmanship inspector was to come. In second grade, we advanced to pens and had inkwells in which to dip them. Now that my motor skills were catching up to my verbal skills, I found cursive relatively easy to learn. At that time, I had long hair, but I don't think it was ever dipped in the inkwell. It was sometimes painfully pulled, though!

In fourth grade, I had the honor of competing in a Cape-wide spelling bee which was broadcast on the Yarmouth radio station WOCB. The other 21 competitors were sixth-graders. Communities then were closely knit; local residents would listen to the broadcast of each round, then stop by the A&P to let my father know how I did. The final round was held at a church hall in Hyannis; three Orleans teachers attended, as well as my mother and my aunt Alice. At last there were only two spellers left standing, myself and a boy from Hyannis. When I misspelled "indelible," my doom was sealed; to lose to a boy was a crushing blow for this early feminist!

My Brownie troop met at the Federated Church of Orleans, which had many beautiful trees and shrubs, most marked with a small sign memorializing a deceased church member. There was also an incinerator out back, so I thought that when someone in the congregation died, he or she was cremated in the incinerator and the ashes interred beneath one of the plantings!

In fifth grade, we moved to a brand-new school building on Eldredge Park Way, while the old school became the Town Hall, a function it still serves today in an updated form. The previous Town Hall had been located in the building which now houses the Academy Playhouse. I remember going there with my mother on voting day and seeing Charlie Sparrow mowing the lawn. The story goes that as a child, he couldn't pronounce Sparrow and would call himself Charlie Ta Pa. The name stuck, and even as a grandfather, he was still known as Charlie Ta Pa!

Fifth grade also marked the year of my transfer to parochial school. St Joan of Arc school was located on Canal Road in Orleans, in the building that now houses the church thrift shop. Students from Orleans and many surrounding Cape towns went to the school. One did not have to be Catholic to attend; Protestant parents could pay tuition to enroll their children, and several did so because they felt that the quality of education was better than in the public schools. The school went through eighth grade, and my class was the first to graduate. I don't think Mother Tharsilla was sorry to see us leave, but Father Lynch was very proud of us and took the whole class out to dinner at the Captain Linnell House.

High school was a different world. The Nauset school system was newly regionalized and included students from Orleans, Eastham, and Wellfleet. Brewster students had a choice of attending either Nauset or Dennis-Yarmouth, while Truro students could go either to Nauset or to Provincetown.

There were a lot of good times: drama club plays; the annual variety show; the student-faculty basketball game with female teachers as cheerleaders; the proms. Our proms were not the sophisticated affairs of today, but I believe we had just as much fun as the current prom goers. The gym was decorated, a band and photographer were hired, and dresses were chosen with much excitement.

Dancing with my date, Dennis Marsh, was an adventure, since he had a penchant for making up his own steps. We finally ended up dancing at arms' length! I still have the wrist corsage he brought me for the junior prom: yellow sweetheart roses with a powder-blue ribbon which matched my dress.

Our senior class trip was a bus excursion to Boston. Dennis had lived in the Boston area and was familiar with the city's sights, so he was able to show me around. We had lunch at Steuben's, went to the top of the old John Hancock building—at that time, the tallest building in Boston—and met a classmate at the Park Square Cinema to see the original "Wuthering Heights." From there we went to the

Saxon Theatre to see "Becket," and then to dinner in Chinatown at Bob Lee's Islander, which had a waterfall in front. The restaurant was known for a cocktail served in a pineapple, so Dennis ordered his non-alcoholic drink that way and later cut up the pineapple for dessert! The food was excellent, and the ladies' room featured a perfume machine, which I thought was the most sophisticated thing in the world.

Big senior privilege: we were allowed to smoke on the bus! How adult we all felt!

Smoking was of course not permitted on school grounds, even at an evening event. A friend earned a two-day suspension for lighting up in the parking lot before a school play.

Another senior privilege was that we were allowed to leave the school premises between final exams. Dennis's family owned a small restaurant nearby, so we would walk down there and have a snack.

None of us worried much about college acceptance or the availability of financial aid, not yet understanding that we were the first wave of the baby boomers and that more students than ever before would be competing with us for those college admissions and scholarships.

It was hard to find the money for college application fees, so I pinned all my hopes on Radcliffe. Surely, I reasoned, as class valedictorian I should have no problem getting in and receiving a scholarship. I overlooked one important fact: most of the other applicants were also valedictorians! I was turned down for early decision but hoped for acceptance in the spring. The letter, when it came, was in a thin envelope, not the plump packet I had expected.

Many of my classmates did not get their first choice of schools, but everyone who wanted to go was accepted somewhere . . . except me. Fortunately, two colleges were still accepting applicants: Bard in New York state and Nasson in southern Maine. I applied to both and was accepted; Bard had already allocated all its financial aid, but Nasson offered me an attractive package.

Radcliffe's rejection turned out to be a blessing in disguise. Nasson was like a family, and the faculty was top-notch. I got a good education there and made friends with whom I am still in touch 50 years later.

Back then, students were often advised to go into teaching because jobs were plentiful. But so many of us took that advice that the jobs became scarcer and scarcer. I had known since my student teaching days that education was not the career for me, but by that time I had invested so much time and effort in training for it that I felt obligated to pursue it. My plan was to use the summers to write, with an eye to becoming famous.

When I finally landed a teaching job, it was in southern Vermont, and homesickness hit hard. I found myself trying to teach French to a class composed of both first-time French students and those who had taken French before and failed it. "What am I doing here?" I asked myself. "I don't even like kids!" One morning I awakened and said, "I'm going to be on Cape Cod before the sun sets!" I broke my contract, resigned, packed my things, and hopped a bus for home.

Finding another job wasn't easy, but eventually I was hired by the Town to work in assessing. I didn't like it, but I learned a lot and met a lot of nice people. I stayed there for nearly 17 years, then left to escape a new supervisor with whom I had a personality conflict. Learning an entirely new career, I entered the insurance profession, got licensed, and earned a designation. Again, I didn't like the industry, but I met a lot of nice people. I was there for 23 years until retiring in 2012. For several years, I also worked evenings and weekends at a bed and breakfast reservation service, and I truly enjoyed matching guests with accommodations that seemed to meet their requirements. I also published two books of poetry.

In 1976, while at Town Hall, I became a justice of the peace to perform marriages and have continued in that capacity for over 40 years. That is another pleasurable activity: no one is happy to see the assessor, and people can be lukewarm about seeing an insurance agent, but everyone is glad to see the wedding officiant!

Many members of my high school graduating class made their lives elsewhere. Some retired here; others have summer homes here; still others visit on occasion; and a few of us chose to stay. Jobs were not easy to come by and did not pay as well as off-Cape employment; if I had not had a family home, I could probably not have afforded to remain on the Cape. I count myself fortunate to have had the opportunity to watch my town evolve, to enjoy its natural beauty, and to give back in small ways to the community. I have been truly blessed.

4

ELAINE'S STORY

During the 1940s, many soldiers were stationed at Camp Wellfleet. When they had a pass, they would often come to Orleans to see a movie, have a soda, and meet girls. Many romances and several marriages resulted. In this story, an Orleans woman's encounter with a soldier presents her with the most difficult decision of her life.

"That was the best one all week!" laughed Elaine Casey as she hung up her headset. "He wanted the number for a Mr. Nickerson on Cape Cod who might be a fisherman!"

"Well, that narrows it down to a few hundred," responded her co-worker Judy Martin. "Nice to end the day with a laugh. Going to the drugstore?"

"Might as well. Joe probably won't be home."

"Working late?"

"Yeah," Elaine sighed. Working on Laura Jackson's bathroom, he said. Working in her bedroom, more likely.

When they arrived at Heath's pharmacy, Judy saw some friends and went to join them. Elaine slid onto the end stool and ordered a coffee frappe. She loved the cheeriness of the soda fountain with its bright posters advertising everything from Coca-Cola to Eskimo Pies.

A few soldiers from Camp Wellfleet came in after the early movie. One approached the stool next to Elaine. "Is this seat taken, ma'am?" he asked in a soft southern drawl.

"No," she said with a smile, liking his courteous manner. "Sit right down."

The soldier looked at the menu. "Excuse me," he said, "What's the difference between a milkshake and a frappe?"

"A milkshake is just milk and syrup. A frappe has ice cream," she answered. "I'm having a frappe."

"Thank you. I think I'll try a chocolate frappe. I'm Steve Brimfield, by the way."

"Elaine Casey. Where are you from?"

"Georgia. Have you ever been there?"

"I've never been south of Connecticut," she said with a laugh.

"You'd like Georgia. There's a lot more to it than peaches and peanuts."

"Do you have a lot of family there?"

"Just my parents and my sister. My dad owns a building supply store. When I get out of the service, I'll join him in the business."

"My husband is in construction. I work at the telephone office." Was it her imagination, or did a shadow cross his face at the mention of the word "husband"?

"The beaches here are nice," he said. "Do you go often?"

"Not that often; I have to admit I can't even swim. But I like to know the ocean is there. I don't think I could live in a landlocked place."

Too soon, it was time for the soldiers to leave. "Good night, Elaine," Steve said. "I hope I'll see you again."

"I hope so too." She felt warmed by the brief encounter with someone who actually seemed interested in what she had to say.

Over the next few weeks, she often saw Steve at the drugstore; when he didn't appear, her disappointment made her annoyed with herself. He always sat with her, sometimes at the counter and sometimes in a booth; she found that she could talk freely and comfortably with him as if with an old friend. Gradually, she confided in him about her marriage.

"Does he ever hit you?" Steve asked, his brow furrowed with concern.

"No, but once he put his fist through the garage door to keep from punching me. Mostly, he yells or makes sarcastic remarks about dumb Cape Codders. He's from the city."

"You deserve better. A lot better."

She smiled ruefully. "Sometimes I think so too."

He rummaged in his pocket for some coins and made a selection from the jukebox: "Inamorata." The look he gave Elaine made her blush and avert her eyes.

One Saturday afternoon, Elaine had finished her errands and decided to stop in at the drugstore for a soda. As she entered, she heard bells and laughter and noticed Laura's sons, Jeff and Tommy, playing pinball. As she turned toward the counter, a couple of other boys came in and greeted the Jacksons.

"Hey," one of them asked, "where'd you get the money to play?"

"Our mom's boyfriend gave it to us," Jeff replied.

"Who's that?"

"A guy named Joe Casey."

Elaine felt as if she had been punched in the stomach. She quickly turned and left the store. Shaking, she sat on a bench and waited for her heart to stop pounding. To suspect it was one thing; to have it confirmed was another. Damn him, she thought, clenching her fists, as the tears oozed out from under her lids.

Then someone was there beside her, slipping an arm around her shoulders. "Elaine," Steve said, "What's wrong?"

She looked up in surprise. "What are you doing here in the daytime?"

"I got a pass and came up on the bus hoping to see you."

"Well, you're seeing me in a sorry state. I just found out for sure that Joe is running around." She told him the story.

"Elaine, you don't have to put up with this. You can get a divorce."

"What would I do then?"

He smiled shyly. "You could marry a soldier who's crazy about you."

She was speechless for a moment. "You . . . you want to marry me?"

"More than anything. I want to take care of you and make you happy. My family would love you as much as I do. You feel the same way about me, don't you?"

Slowly, she nodded. "Yes. I've been fighting it because I'm married. I promised to stick with him for better or for worse, and Lord knows, this is worse."

"I don't think loyalty means accepting mistreatment. It's a two-way street, and he hasn't upheld his end of the bargain. I have to ship out next week, but I'll give you an address where you can write to me. Please let me know as soon as possible what you decide to do."

Over the next week, Elaine found it hard to focus on work. Could she really leave the place that was so much a part of her? She loved Steve, but she had loved Joe in the beginning; maybe part of her still did, or his betrayal wouldn't have hurt her so deeply. And she also loved her little town with its harbor and seagulls and the salt tang in the air when the wind was right. She was part of it, and it was part of her.

In the mail one day, she received an envelope with a Georgia postmark, but addressed in a feminine handwriting. Inside was a letter from Steve's sister, Ginny. "Steve has told us all about you," she wrote. "He's happier than he's ever been. I hope to have the pleasure of welcoming you to the family." The warm tone brought tears to Elaine's eyes. How could she not go? She would tell Joe the next day, when she wasn't scheduled to work.

Joe came home for lunch in a grouchy mood. "That damn Paul messed up again," he complained. "Typical ass-backward Cape Codder."

Elaine took a deep breath. "Well, this Cape Codder's ass is going forward," she said. "I'm leaving you, Joe."

He stared at her. "What the hell do you mean?"

"Just what I said. I know about Laura, and I know she isn't the first. I've met someone who appreciates me, and I'm not wasting any more of my life on you." She related the pinball story.

His eyes widened, then he forced a laugh. "Those dumb kids! I gave them money because I felt sorry for them; I don't think they've had much fun since their father died. But I'm not their mother's boyfriend . . . or anyone else's."

"I might have believed you, Joe," she replied. "But that was the day you supposedly went to New Bedford with Charlie Snow."

"You've got the day wrong."

"The only thing I got wrong was the man I married."

To her amazement, his eyes filled with tears. "I know I haven't always done right, but I'll make it up to you. Don't leave me."

"Too little, too late," she said. "I'm going."

"I'll be right back," he said in a choked voice. "Don't move."

Where had he gone, she wondered. To get Laura to corroborate his innocence?

In five minutes he was back, with—oh, Lord—Elaine's mother. "Talk to her, Ma," he begged. "Tell her not to leave me."

Her mother sat down. "Elaine," she began, "you don't know this man very well. And suppose you don't like it down South?"

"You knew about this guy?" Joe burst out. "Why didn't you tell me?"

"Because Elaine is my daughter," she replied calmly. "And you haven't been much of a husband."

Joe hung his head. "I know," he said sadly, "I'm sorry. I'm asking for a second chance."

"Elaine," her mother went on, "you won't know anyone down there. If anything goes wrong, you'll have no one to turn to. Here, you have your brother and sister and me, and all your friends. This is your home. Don't get yourself into something you'll regret."

Confused and weary, Elaine burst into tears. "Leave me alone," she sobbed. "Both of you, just leave me alone." She went into the bedroom and slammed the door.

About fifteen minutes later, she heard the car leaving and looked out the window to make sure her mother was with Joe. Then she left the house and started walking. Faster and faster she walked, until her breath came in gasps. She was headed for the place where she always found peace: the town cemetery. She had always found its aura of history and continuity soothing. Past old graves and new she walked, past stones with familiar names, some of them relatives: Doane, Snow, Crosby, Nickerson. At the top of the hill, she stopped to catch her breath and sat on the stone bench marking the graves of a Midwestern family who had relocated to the Cape. They had had money, but their wealth had not exempted them from tragedy; one son had died in a plane crash, another had taken his own life.

As she sat there, trying to make sense of her thoughts and feelings, she noticed the copper dome of the Congregational church. When she was a child, she had thought the dome was solid gold. All her memories lived in this town; could she make new ones in another place? And did she truly love Steve, or was she just grateful for his attentiveness? She gradually realized that the sun was setting; the sky turned a luminous pink. Suddenly she was aware of another presence. "Elaine," said Joe in a husky voice, "Can I sit with you?" She nodded.

"How did you know where I was?"

"I drove all over town looking for you, and then I remembered how you always liked it here. I parked down by the entrance and walked up, hoping I'd find you."

"Well, you found me."

"Elaine, I've been a damned fool. I don't deserve you, but I still love you, whether you believe it or not, and I want another chance to prove it. Can you give me that chance?"

"Why should I?"

"Look at that sky. It reminds me of the day we drove through Harwich after the snowstorm; the snow-covered tree branches were so pretty against the pink sky. I'd like to have more rides like that with you, and only with you."

"Joe," she said, "I'm not sure if I can ever trust you or love you again, but I'll have to give it a try because this is my home and I can't bear to leave it."

"I can't ask for more than that." He held out his hand. "Let's go home."

They walked down the hill together as the pink sky faded into dusk.

5

PEG

This story is loosely based on a memory of my mother's about an acquaintance whose unconventional marriage to a man with divided loyalties had a tragic ending.

*P*eg Potter wiped down the counter at the Orleans Cafe. Her shift was nearly over and her boyfriend, Ken Crawford, would be coming to pick her up.

Sam Sears, a local fisherman, came in for his usual BLT. "Pretty peppy Peggy Potter," he greeted her.

"Silly salty Sammy Sears," she responded with a grin and a shake of her red curls.

"Where's your sweetie?"

"He'll be along."

"Well, don't forget to invite me when the big day arrives," he teased.

If the big day arrives, she thought sadly. Ken's mother wouldn't exactly welcome her to the family. She was frostily polite to Peg, but it was obvious that she disapproved of their relationship . . . or maybe of Ken's having a girlfriend at all. People thought Peg had it made, dating a rich guy, but it was his mother who held the purse strings. A heart murmur had kept him out of the Army and he had gone to art school, but he didn't want to teach, and it was hard for an artist to make a living, so he had to dance to the maternal tune.

Peg's worries faded as she saw Ken's baby blue convertible pull up. She felt a smile spreading across her face at the sight of his tall frame unfolding from the driver's seat.

She removed her apron and went outside. Ken swept her into a bear hug, lifting her off her feet. "Great news," he said. "I've landed a show at the Skaket Gallery in another month!"

"Wonderful! That's so exciting! I know art is your passion."

"One of my two passions. The other is right beside me. And speaking of passion . . ."

On the evening of the opening reception, Peg waited nervously for Ken and his mother to pick her up. Her stomach had been churning for days at the thought of attending the reception with Mrs. Crawford. She hoped her simple peach dress would be appropriate.

Walking to Ken's car, Peg nearly stumbled in the heels she seldom had occasion to wear. Claire Crawford sat regally in the front passenger seat, dressed in an impeccably tailored grey suit with pearls. "Hello, Margaret," she said. "My, aren't you brave to wear that color with your hair!"

Meow, thought Peg, but she forced a smile. "It's nice to see you, Mrs. Crawford," she lied.

The gallery owner, Douglas Taylor, greeted them warmly. Ken's works were beautifully displayed on two walls. Peg was immediately drawn to a painting of a young woman with copper curls and green eyes. Could it be? Ken nodded and her own eyes grew misty.

Other people began to filter in. Peg was surprised to see Sam Sears. "What's that fisherman doing here?" Mrs. Crawford asked disdainfully. "I invited him," Ken replied. "He's a nice guy and a smart one."

Peg suddenly felt faint. Her knees were about to buckle when Ken caught her elbow. Sam hurried over to help.

"I'm all right," she assured them. "It's just a little stuffy in here. I need some air."

"I'll give you a ride home," Sam offered. "Ken will be anchored here for a while."

She said little on the short drive and was grateful that Sam didn't ask questions. "I'd feel sick myself if I had to be around Mrs. Crabgrass very long," he quipped.

As Peg stretched out on the sofa, she tried to push away the thought that kept intruding: that there was a likely cause for the nausea and the faintness.

Ken called later that night to check on her. "I'm better," she said, "but I'm going to call in sick tomorrow just to be on the safe side. I need to talk to you. Can you come over around ten?"

"I'll be there."

Ken arrived bearing a bag of blueberry muffins fresh from the bakery. "Oh Ken," Peg said, "that's so sweet. But I can't eat anything. Maybe some tea and toast later."

Understanding dawned on his face. "Are you—are we—is it?"

"I think so."

"Well, it looks like we've got a wedding to plan."

"Your mother will never accept it. She thinks I'm not good enough for you."

"She wouldn't think the Queen of Sheba was good enough. But this will be her grandchild. She isn't a monster, Peg. She's never recovered from losing my dad; that's why she holds onto me so tightly. Let's go talk to her right now and try to get her on our side."

Mrs. Crawford received the news more calmly than Peg had anticipated. "Well, Kenneth," she sighed, "I had hoped you would have better sense than to get yourself trapped."

"I'm not trying to trap anybody!" Peg burst out.

"Be that as it may," Mrs. Crawford continued, "the child will be a Crawford. Make your own wedding arrangements; I shall not be attending."

"When can Peg move in?" Ken asked.

"There will be no question of her moving in."

"But her apartment isn't big enough for both of us and a baby."

"In that case, Kenneth, you are welcome to remain here. Indeed, I would prefer it."

"Mrs. Crawford," cried Peg, "why do you hate me?"

The older woman regarded her impassively. "I don't hate you, Margaret. I simply don't think you will be a suitable wife for my son."

"Isn't that my decision, Mother?" retorted Ken.

"Of course, just as it is my decision as to how my money is to be spent. The child's needs will be provided for, and an educational trust fund will be available as long as his or her surname is not changed."

"Why would it change?" they both asked simultaneously.

"I envision a quiet divorce in the not too distant future, and Margaret may wish to remarry." She rose. "Now, if you'll excuse me, I'm hosting the garden club luncheon today." And she was gone.

"Oh my God," whispered Peg, leaning into Ken.

"She'll come around. Let's go apply for our license."

Peg had a much warmer reception at her parents' house that night. "Oh honey," Grace Potter said. "You know we'll help in any way we can. I'll take care of the baby when you go back to work."

"If you ask me," Albert Potter opined, "that boy should get a real job and get out from under his mother's thumb. He'd make more money painting houses than pictures."

"Oh Dad," said Peg, "I couldn't ask him to do that. He'd only end up resenting me."

"Then he wouldn't be much of a husband," her father muttered.

When people noticed Peg's wedding ring and offered congratulations, she smiled and thanked them. Sam said nothing and she was grateful for his silence, although as her pregnancy advanced, he often asked how she was feeling.

Ken spent as much time with her as he could, but it didn't feel like a real marriage, and she was more frustrated than she would acknowledge.

Megan Elisabeth Crawford arrived with Peg's flaming hair and Ken's cool blue eyes. Even his mother had to admit she was a little beauty, "although the red hair is too bad. Perhaps it will darken as she grows older." Ken was besotted with her and made a project of "The Megan Series": charcoal sketches, pastel portraits, watercolor and oil paintings of the little girl at various stages of growth. Peg adored her daughter and enjoyed showing her off. Sam welcomed her with his typical humor: "Peg and Meg/Are you pulling my leg?" Peg responded with a laugh, "You're not a poet/And you should know it!"

Although Megan was growing and changing every day, her parents' relationship was not. Peg found it increasingly difficult to respond to Ken's romantic overtures. "Where's my loving wife?" he teased.

"Looking for a loving marriage!" she exclaimed bitterly. "I want a husband, not a guest!"

The arguments grew more frequent, and Peg began to wonder if Mrs. Crawford's prediction of a divorce had been right. The older woman could live for decades longer, and Peg didn't want to spend those decades in a part-time marriage.

One evening when Megan was two years old, Ken stopped by to
see her and to show Peg his latest sketch of the little girl.
"Tomorrow is supposed to be beautiful," he said. "I'm going to
meet Rob and Stan at Eldredge Field and play a little baseball."

"Be careful of your hands," Peg warned. "You can't do much
painting with a broken finger."

"Don't worry," he said. "I've got a good sturdy catcher's mitt. I
haven't played ball in a long time, and I miss it."

The following day as she chatted with her boss, Frank, during a
rare quiet moment, Peg was surprised to see Ken's buddy Rob
Stevens come running in, out of breath and sweating. "Oh God,
Peg," he gasped, leaning against the counter as tears ran down his
face. "It's Ken. The ball hit him right over the heart."

"Is he in the hospital?"

Rob shook his head sadly, unable to meet her eyes. "He's gone."

She stared at him numbly. It wasn't possible; it wasn't right.
Time seemed to have stopped.

Frank took her gently by the shoulders and guided her into the
office. "Sit here while I call your dad to come and get you," he said.

Her parents kept Megan overnight while Peg attempted to sort
through her feelings. She was a widow, but had she ever really been
a wife? Oh God, she would have to call Ken's mother. The next
morning, her fingers trembled as she dialed the number. Marie, the
housekeeper, answered. "Peg," she said gently, "Mrs. Crawford
asked me to tell you that the arrangements are taken care of and that
Megan will be provided for. She said she doesn't want to be
disturbed. I'm so sorry for your loss; he was a sweet boy."

"Yes, he was," Peg agreed. "Thank you, Marie." So, she would
have to learn the funeral arrangements from the newspaper like
everyone else.

The obituary made no mention of Peg or Megan. Funeral
services were to be private, but there would be a visitation.

Peg's parents offered to accompany her to the funeral home, but she declined. "I have to do this on my own," she said. The short walk would give her some time to gather her courage.

As she approached the white clapboard building, her resolve suddenly deserted her. She paced back and forth, trying to muster the nerve to face Mrs. Crawford.

Sam Sears came out the front door and spoke to her. "Want me to go in with you?" he asked.

"Thanks, but this is something I have to do by myself." She smiled ruefully.

"I'll wait and take you home."

The funeral home was crowded and Peg felt claustrophobic. She stood in line with the other mourners and eventually reached her mother-in-law. Claire Crawford glared at her coldly. "If not for you," she said in a low voice, "he might still be alive."

"I couldn't have kept him from playing baseball," Peg replied in astonishment.

"Nor could I, but his heart didn't need the stress he's been under. Please pay your respects and leave."

Peg walked shakily toward the casket and gazed at her husband, handsome even in death. She slipped quickly out the side door as the tears started.

Sam appeared at her side and gently guided her to his car. "Sorry I'm such a wreck," she said, striving to regain control.

"You're entitled. I give you credit for dealing with that old battle-ax on your own."

"At least I have Ken's daughter."

"You'll have his artwork too."

"How do you know?"

"I witnessed the will. Ken wasn't naïve; he knew he wouldn't live forever, and he knew the art should belong to you and Meg. My guess is that the stuff is going to be valuable someday; the guy had talent."

Peg drew a shaky breath. The tears were threatening again. Trying for a light note, she asked, "How come you always show up when I need a friend?"

His face was solemn. "If you don't know by now . . ."

"But . . . you never said anything."

"I liked Ken. And I didn't think I had a chance anyway. I know you didn't care about the money, but he was educated and cultured. While he was making art, I was digging clams."

"Artists couldn't create if they didn't eat," she reminded him.

"Guess you're right."

"Sam," she said hesitantly, "I have a lot of things to sort out before I can even begin to think about caring for someone again. But if you want to wait . . ."

He smiled. "I'm not going anywhere."

She smiled back. "Neither am I."

ABOUT THE AUTHOR

Mary E. McDermott is a 13th-generation Cape Codder living in Orleans. She worked for 17 years in the Orleans Assessor's Office and 23 years as a commercial insurance broker at Pike Insurance Agency. She has been a justice of the peace to solemnize marriages since 1976 and has previously published two books of poetry, *Tapestry* and *Handle with Care*. Her poems have appeared in several publications including the *Christian Science Monitor*.

ABOUT THE PRESS

Sea Crow Press
amplifying voices

Sea Crow Press is named for a flock of five talkative crows you can find on the beach anywhere between Scupper Lane and Bone Hill Road in Barnstable Village on Cape Cod.

According to Norse legend, one-eyed Odin sent two crows out into the world so they could return and tell him its stories. If you sit and listen to the sea crows in Barnstable as they fly and roost and chatter, it's an easy legend to believe.

Operating from the premise that the small press plays an essential part in contemporary arts by amplifying its voices, Sea Crow Press is committed to building an accessible community of writers and dedicated to telling stories that matter. *Old Orleans: Memories of a Cape Cod Town*, is its second Cape-themed offering.

www.seacrowpress.com